ROOTS & WINGS

WORKBOOK

for use with the compact disc or audio-cassette

ROOTS & WINGS –

Guided imagery and meditations to transform your life

PUJA THOMSON

Roots & Wings Workbook - guided imagery and meditations to transform your life. (1999)   ISBN 1-928663-00 -1
Roots & Wings CD - guided imagery and meditations to transform your life (1999)   ISBN 1-928663-01-X
Roots & Wings Cassette - guided imagery and meditations to transform your life (1996)   ISBN 1-928663-02-8
Roots & Wings Workbook and CD - guided imagery and meditations to transform your life   ISBN 1-928663-03-6
Roots & Wings Workbook and Cassette -guided imagery and meditations to transform your life ISBN 1-928663-04-4

1. Self-help, 2. Family and Relationships, 3. Body, Mind and Spirit

WORKBOOK
Concept and Words - Puja Thomson © 1999
Published by - ROOTS & WINGS, New Paltz NY
Printed in the United States of America by – MORRIS PUBLISHING, 3212 East Highway 30, Kearney NE 68847

AUDIO
Words - PUJA THOMSON © 1996,
Music - RICHARD SHULMAN © 1996
Production - ROOTS & WINGS, New Paltz NY
Engineer - SCOTT PETITO, NRS Studios, Hurley NY
Manufacturer - MAGNETIC NORTH AUDIO, Saugerties NY

ARTWORK
Logo - HELENE SARKIS, Glen Cove NY
Cover art - NANCY OSTROVSKY, Kerhonkson NY
Photo - ALICE SU, New York NY
Graphics - THE TURNING MILL, Palenville NY

TABLE OF CONTENTS

iv

WELCOME TO ROOTS & WINGS

INTRODUCTION

*" There are only two lasting bequests we may give ourselves and our children,
one is roots - the other, wings"- Anonymous*

Roots and wings

We all have many roots - some nourish, others strangle - and we long for the joy of taking wing. Harnessing the power of our roots and our wings can bring about dramatic transformation. *Roots* symbolize nourishment from the earth and groundedness. *Wings* symbolize flying, lightness and expansion. Roots and wings are wonderful images from nature. Together, they support our growth, reminding us of our capacity for regeneration and transformation.

Over the years I have observed, in myself and in others, the beauty of deep nourishing roots and strong flexible wings. I've also felt the pain of compacted roots that bind, roots that can't get a hold in rough terrain or rootlessness, and the fragility of weakened wings, whether clipped or broken. We can all benefit from being well rooted so that we can fly freely.

The *ROOTS & WINGS* concept, audio and workbook have grown out of over thirty years' experience as a therapist and spiritual counselor, from my love of nature and from my inner and outer journeys while living in different cultures. In bringing insights from these sources I guide you, as I do in my work, to plant your feet firmly on the ground and connect to the nourishing replenishing energy of the earth. Just as the roots of a plant or tree are essential for growth, so grounding will strengthen your foundation in life. Using the imagery of healthy roots is a powerful way to redress early imbalances or neglect and can help you grow beyond the limitations of your past.

I also guide you to appreciate the gift of wings in your life. Strengthening your wings will help you to rise off the ground, soaring to gain a new, higher perspective. Using your pictures of strong flexible wings will help you lighten up so you can take off with confidence, trusting your own abilities.

Our past is valuable and can be recycled for new growth

I grew up in Scotland, a country where the perspective goes deep into the past, and where strong tenacious roots often bind people to the traditional. I was the "minister's daughter" and one of the "Thomson twins" in a small country market town. This gave me a solid foundation in my family and culture. Yet its clear-cut rules of right and wrong didn't always support creative individuality. I needed to be in touch with a sense of my own inner roots before I could branch out – first to experience how people lived in other countries of Europe and in India, and later to test and strengthen my wings by coming to live in America.

Your story may be very different. Even the most negative family experiences provide a framework for personal exploration and spiritual growth, and can be recycled like compost to produce nutrients for new growth. As an example, a young woman, whom I'll call Mary, experienced much uprooting in her early life. When her mother died, she was sent to her grandparents then, in turn, to an aunt and a foster home. She was very unhappy since no one could fill her mother's shoes. She increasingly kept others at a distance and, as a result, she never felt well-enough nourished until she learned at a workshop to ground herself on a daily basis. The more Mary planted her feet on the earth and visualized her roots like those of a great tree, the more comfort and strength she felt. With the help of explorations offered in Part One of the workbook, she found a way to make up for her early deprivation and, from then on, was able to review, reframe, rework and recreate her life.

Connection to Spirit supports transformation

When we honor our inner, intuitive, spiritual roots and wings, and welcome Divine power into our lives, we strengthen our core essence. Knowing that each of us is a child of the Universe, and not just a child of our birth parents, is greatly affirming as we journey through life's changing seasons. Mark, one of my clients, unexpectedly found this to be true. As an adolescent, he had rejected all "punitive religious dogma" and, for forty years, he had paid scant attention to things spiritual. To his surprise, tears began to well up when he first heard the words of The Invocation. ("…Honor Great Spirit, Creative Source of Light and Life in the Universe. Ask for a blessing from Great Spirit to surround you…") His deep longing surfaced and his soul was nourished by a new understanding of the Divine as he participated in the explorations of Part Two.

Your unique life matters

We are living at a pivotal time in history, making a shift from one millenium to another. More than ever the balancing energy of earth and sky is needed – nourishment to ground and feed us and winds of change to encourage us to live creatively and compassionately as humans.

We are all children of Mother Earth. Yet like snowflakes, no two of us are alike. Whatever your upbringing, your unique life is a gift and challenge. The audio and workbook will help you become more grounded, receiving nourishment from the best of your roots, and will help you develop the confidence and strength to fly in accordance with your own gifts and vision. Like a pebble thrown in the water, your creativity will ripple outwards, adding to harmony, unity, and peace on the earth.

"Once roots are there, your wings will reach to the highest sky possible" –Osho

THE COMPACT DISC / AUDIO-CASSETTE *

Guided imagery and meditations to transform your life

ROOTS & WINGS is many faceted. It takes you from the past, through the present, into the future, with words and music created for strength and freedom. Relaxation, music, meditation and guided imagery, especially from nature, when combined together with your intention, are powerful tools for bringing change. Throughout the audio you'll hear my voice weaving these elements together and you'll be shown how to use these tools as basic building blocks for your transformation.

I make clear suggestions, so that all you need to do is make yourself comfortable and receptive as you listen. Let the tone of my voice, and the music, carry you into your personal journey.

Two complementary approaches to personal transformation

Each part of the audio, lasting just under thirty minutes, has a different focus. Together they form a coherent whole, yet it is also easy and fruitful to listen to shorter portions when you feel so inclined.

Part One: Healing your past

Here you learn how to become centered, with an awareness of your roots and your wings, before you travel back to discover what was really important to you as a child. Your past is the stuff of which you are made. You can use whatever has been passed on to you from your family and culture, building on even the negative parts, to redesign your present and create your future. You are guided to release the hold of roots that are destructive, turn limitations into blessings, and honor and carry forward the best of your roots. _(Tracks 1-5 / Side A)_

Part Two: Connecting to your spiritual roots and wings

This half provides meditations and visualizations to strengthen your roots and spread you wings by affirming your spiritual alignment in life. You are guided from your external concerns to an inner sacred space in which you can re-connect with the Greater Whole, honor Divine Power, rekindle trust in your inner guidance, appreciate blessings, and manifest your dreams. _(Tracks 6-12 / Side B)_

---

* Hereafter referred to as 'the audio'.

THE WORKBOOK

The workbook is a tool to support your commitment to transformation
While listening to the audio alone is very effective, using the workbook enriches your experience and deepens your inner dialogue. It is organized in three sections:

Welcome to Roots & Wings
The introductory section presents the concept underlying my work, a brief overview of the audio and workbook, and practical information that is helpful as you work with both.

Roots & Wings for Transformation
This section lies at the heart of the workbook. Its simple step-by step sequence gives a framework for your active participation. Yet, at any point, you can follow your own intuition:
- Step One: Listen to the audio.
- Step Two: Use the *Day-to-Day* pages along with the audio.
- Step Three: Use the *In-depth Insight* pages along with the audio.

The *Day-to-Day* and *In-depth Insight* transformation pages with their open-ended suggestions invite your response. These have been refined from use by numerous clients and workshop participants.

The *Day-to-Day* pages include an introductory page to capture your first impressions of listening to the audio, pivotal pages for ongoing use with Parts One and Two, and three additional pages - for your memories, comments and occasional review.

The *In-depth Insight* pages present the text of the audio, a detailed commentary, and suggestions designed to take you step by step, in more depth, through each of the guided imagery or meditation explorations.

Additional Resources
The final part of the workbook includes an explanation of how relaxation, guided imagery, meditation, music, journal writing, and strong feelings can assist you as you use the audio and workbook. It lists books, tapes, CDs and other general information.

HOW TO USE THE AUDIO AND WORKBOOK: HELPFUL HINTS and PRACTICAL SUGGESTIONS

Quality time
Create personal quality time by putting aside times during the week, or better still each day, to re-create yourself. Using the audio and workbook regularly will lead to relaxation, insight and transformation.

A quiet space
Just as plants flourish in a pleasant environment, so do we. It is important to create a restful space for yourself. Look for an environment that is conducive to peace and quiet, with as few distractions as possible. Turn off the telephone, shut your door and, if there are others around, ask not to be disturbed.

A three step program
If you are not sure how to proceed, think of yourself embarking on a three-step program. Take time to repeat each step regularly for as long as it has meaning for you and you are making discoveries. Only then, go on to the next step.

Step One - use the audio in your own way
ROOTS & WINGS has many sections, with much to discover in its two complementary approaches to transformation. Many people have found that listening to Part One *(Healing Your Past)* and Part Two *(Connecting to Your Spiritual Roots and Wings)* in an ongoing rhythm provides a good balance. Others have felt an intuitive preference to engage more consistently with one part rather than the other. Consider listening to the entire audio several times, then tune into yourself to sense whether you are drawn more to Part One or Part Two. If so, use the sequence that feels comfortable for you, without feeling obligated to follow the order presented. Trust your inclination. You can always go back to the other part later when it feels right.

Listen to the audio repeatedly
With some explorations, daily repetition enables you to become more centered in a shorter period of time and builds your inner strength. *The Daily Alignment* and *The Invocation* will be very helpful in centering you, especially at the beginning of the day or at times when you feel out of balance, worried or just plain tired.

Frequent use of the audio, or parts of the audio, also allows you to focus on small units of your experience at a time so that different memories and aspects can surface. This is especially true in *Your Family and Lineage.* Don't try to capture everything at once. It's more important to relax as much as you can while listening. You may find that half an hour a day works well or that you prefer an hour, or more, a few times a week.

Steps Two and Three - use the transformation pages along with the audio
After a period of listening, you will find it beneficial to record your experience by writing comments or drawing pictures in your workbook. The transformation (*Day-to-Day* and *In-*

depth Insight) pages provide suggestions to help you express your feelings and note your thoughts, memories and aspirations, as you would in a journal. This allows you to acknowledge and clarify your insights both at the time you write and when you read your notes again at a future date. Knowing that you have a place to record even the slightest hint of a memory or an insight can help you relax. It is helpful to keep some colored pencils, crayons or even paints beside your workbook, to use creatively and spontaneously.

Start your journal work with the first *Day-to-Day* page of **Step Two** - *My First Impressions*. Then use the pivotal pages for Part One and Part Two for a while along with the pages for *memories, comments* and occasional *tuning in*. When you wish to pursue a specific theme in more depth, gain more insight, or if you wish guidelines to use with a group of friends, turn to **Step Three** - the *In-depth Insight* pages. There is no right or wrong way to use your workbook. Your particular insights and creativity will help you to use your pages in your own unique way.

Use the pause button
If you need to take time to be with yourself and your feelings at any point, push the pause button to turn off the sound until you are ready to continue. Sometimes you will want to integrate what you have received, write in your workbook or just be with your feelings, your memories or your inner guidance. It is important for your ongoing process that you take time out to linger, acknowledge and release your feelings, and not rush on before you are truly ready.

A note about parents, caregivers and families
For purposes of clarity, please note that I refer to "parents" and "family" in the broadest sense. With increasing divorce rates, one-parent and blended families, family life can less and less be described as the old two-parent norm. I recognize that, for very many of you, your parents may not be your blood parents, and your family may have consisted of an uncle or aunt, grandparents, same sex parents, or other children and adult caregivers in a group setting. When you read or hear the word "parent" or "family", please let your memories take you to the truth of your experience as a child - whatever that was. Let yourself also gravitate to the names you used as a child, perhaps the more familiar "dad", "pop", or first name of your parent.

Caution: Please do not listen to the audio while driving
As you transition safely to a more diffuse inner focus by listening to the music and my voice, you may experience a dreamy kind of awareness. Obviously this is dangerous for driving or doing tasks for which you need alert attention.

*If you are not familiar with how relaxation, guided imagery, meditation, music, journal writing, or strong feelings can be used for healing and to enhance your growth, please turn now to these topics in **Thoughts To Help You On Your Journey** at the beginning of **Additional Resources**. Otherwise continue directly to the transformation pages.*

ROOTS&WINGS™

FOR

TRANSFORMATION

STEP 1: LISTEN TO THE AUDIO

CHART OF THE AUDIO

Become familiar with the audio

As you relax and let the words and music seep in, you will begin to activate a response from deep within yourself. This chart provides the CD track numbers along with a short description for easy navigation. Listen as often as you like. The timing (in parenthesis in minutes and seconds) is accurate for the CD, and varies slightly for the tape.

PART ONE : HEALING YOUR PAST

1. **Introduction (3:38):** Provides the creative concept and practical information.

2. **Roots and Wings (6:40):** Leads to a discovery of your roots and wings in current time.

3. **Daily Alignment-1 (3:55):** Provides strength to create change in your life now through grounding and breath work.

4. **Your Family and Lineage (10:13):** Guides your journey to the past. Discover the thread of what was really important to you as a child as memories, stories, and feelings surface.

5. **Transforming Your Past (4:22):** Invites you to rework the effects of your childhood roots - release whatever invalidates you, recognize blessings in limitations, and deepen your connection to whatever nourishes you.

PART TWO: CONNECTING TO YOUR SPIRITUAL ROOTS & WINGS

6. **Introduction to Part Two and to the Invocation (1:17)**

7. **Invocation and Blessing (2:57):** Enables you to center yourself as part of the Greater Whole and to honor the Divine Power in your life. It guides you from your external concerns to an inner sacred space.

8. **Daily Alignment -2 (3:22):** Offers you a second version of centering and grounding to reinforce your earlier experience.

9. **Being in this Moment (1:57):** Invites you to listen to any messages that come from deep within.

10. **The Rooted One's Growth and the Winged One's Flight (10:13):** Brings awareness of the cycles and seasons of your life, where you are now, what is needed for your further growth. Call forth a winged one for guidance.

11. **The Universe's Abundant Gifts (3:38):** Renews you as you recall blessings, large and small, past and present, that you have received from many sources.

12. **Birthing Your Dreams (5:29):** Affirms your intention to bring forth to the light, the hope, dream or wish that has been gestating within you.

FOR

TRANSFORMATION

STEP 2: USE THE DAY-TO-DAY JOURNAL PAGES

DAY-TO-DAY JOURNAL PAGES

Step Two's *Day-to-Day* pages are pivotal for your transformation
They include one introductory page to get you started, and seven pages for ongoing use.

- *My First Impressions,* the introductory page, is where you can express your initial experiences of listening to the audio, *even* if you are not yet ready to use the other *Day-to-Day* pages.

- *Roots for Strength and Nourishment* enables you to record your experiences and summarize the insights you gain as you become grounded and make choices to heal your past, using Part One of the audio.

- *Wings for Flight and Freedom* enables you to record your experiences and summarize the insights you gain and the choices you make, as you deepen your spiritual life and spread your wings, using Part Two of the audio.

- *My Memories* is the place to gather memories from the past when you wish to track them as they emerge. Log them as you choose - briefly or with many details.

- *My Comments* is where you can let your thoughts, impressions, insights and feelings flow freely.

- *Tuning into Myself* offers suggestions for those times when you wish to review your progress - for example, when you have completed a natural cycle of using the previous pages.

Start using the pivotal pages as soon as you are ready, and return to them time after time. This will help you build a strong foundation and offer a different perspective as your personal process unfolds. *Each day, choose a ROOTS page, a WINGS page, or do both!* Select the open-ended suggestions that work for you. You don't have to complete all of them. When a memory surfaces from your past, use a *MEMORY* page. At any time you wish, use a *COMMENTS* page. After working with the *DAY-TO-DAY* pages for a while, use a *TUNING INTO MYSELF* page.

For further guidance, please turn to *On Journaling* on page 69 and, from time to time, review *Welcome to Roots and Wings.*

When you are ready to move on, weave in and out of your Day-to-Day pages forward to the In-depth Insight pages.

Day-to-Day Page 1

today's date_____

MY FIRST IMPRESSIONS
For use after listening to the audio

LET YOUR FIRST RESPONSES FLOW FREELY FROM YOUR HEAD AND HEART through your hand onto the paper - communicating to and from your inner self.

Note your feelings, thoughts, impressions, longings, uncertainties, unexpected connections, insights . . .

Note how the music and the tone of the spoken words affect you . . .

Note any words, phrases or explorations that particularly resonate within you in some way -

> *Those that stir things up or challenge you . . .*

> *Those that calm, center or comfort you . . .*

Note any themes that intrigue you or that you'd like to explore more . . .

Day-to-Day Page 2

ROOTS FOR STRENGTH AND NOURISHMENT
For use with Part One

GROUNDING AND CENTERING

My roots are . . . Describe or draw your images and feelings.

Slowing down to receive the life-force energy of earth helps me to . . .

Once I feel well-grounded, I can also breathe in Life's Spirit and remember my wings . . .
This centering helps me to . . .

RECONNECTING TO MY CHILDHOOD ROOTS

I recall these memories about myself, my family or ancestors . . . (Highlights here and log details on your Memories Page)

Day-to-Day Page 3

today's date_____

ROOTS FOR STRENGTH AND NOURISHMENT *(continued)*

RECONNECTING TO MY CHILDHOOD ROOTS *(continued)*

The thread from my past that's especially important to me . . .

CHOOSING TO HEAL AND TRANSFORM MY PAST

I release . . .

The negative experience or limitation I am now able to see as a gift is . . .

I recognize, celebrate and give thanks for this blessing . . .

Day-to-Day Page 4

today's date_____

WINGS FOR FLIGHT AND FREEDOM
For use with Part Two

HONORING THE DIVINE

Reconnecting to the web of light and life to which I belong, I experience . . .

Deepening my centering and truly listening to myself, I become aware of . . .

MY INNER JOURNEY

As "the rooted one", I grew into . . . (Describe or draw your images past and present)

facing these challenges . . .

My emergence as "the winged one" was like. . . Describe or draw your images and feelings

Day-to-Day Page 5

WINGS FOR FLIGHT AND FREEDOM (continued)

MY INNER JOURNEY (continued)
In the circle of love between the winged one (my higher self) and the rooted one (my everyday self), I receive this message . . .

NOURISHMENT FROM MANY SOURCES

Recognizing many blessings, past and present, I specifically acknowledge . . .

The hope, dream or wish I choose to empower is . . .

I give wings to my prayer that . . .

Day-to-Day Page 6

today's date_____

MY MEMORIES

TODAY I REMEMBER . . .

Day-to-Day Page 7

*today's date*_____

MY COMMENTS

TODAY I AM AWARE OF . . .   (*feelings, thoughts, impressions, insights*)

Day-to-Day Page 8

*today's date*_____

TUNING INTO MYSELF

WHAT IS MY NEXT STEP?
Sense whether you are at the beginning of a cycle, somewhere in the middle, or coming to the end of a phase on your journey. Note where you are, how you feel and what you might do next. Trust your sense of what's right for you.

You may feel that you have extracted enough for now - or perhaps you'd like to listen without writing in your journal or workbook for a while - or may be you want to focus on one portion of the audio or . . .

If you find you are ready or eager to go on the adventure of rooting deeper or flying higher, at this point turn to the IN-DEPTH INSIGHT PAGES.

FOR

TRANSFORMATION

STEP 3: USE THE IN-DEPTH INSIGHT PAGES

THE *IN-DEPTH INSIGHT* PAGES

The trio of text, commentary and transformation pages
Step Three enables you to root deeper, and fly higher, exploration by exploration.

- The text is included in fine print within the bordered inserts for those times when you wish clarification of the spoken word.

- The commentary elaborates on the theme or themes of each section.

- The *In-depth Insight* pages help to record your experiences and clarify your insights and choices, one exploration at a time. While it is usual to record what has happened to you in the past tense, experiment with writing in the present tense especially when you are in touch with new insights and understandings. Doing so makes the process more immediate.

For further guidance, turn to *On Journaling* on page 69 and, from time to time, review the information in *Welcome to Roots and Wings*.

Weave in and out of your In-depth Insight pages back to your Day-to-Day journal pages and into your life in your own way.

INTRODUCTION

YOUR UNIQUE LIFE MATTERS

Text of audio: Track 1

Hello! This CD / tape is about the power of your roots and your wings!

ROOTS speak to us of nourishment from the earth and groundedness. WINGS speak to us of flying, and of lightness and expansion. As we prepare for a new millennium, it is time to honor the balancing nourishment of earth and sky in our lives. The astronauts' incredible photography from space has already given us a new view of our 'home planet'. We have seen that we all live together on one sphere. Though culturally diverse, we are all children of this Mother Earth. So whatever your upbringing, your unique life is a gift and challenge at this time!

My name is Puja Thomson, and I've created this CD / tape to support you in the inner work of transforming your life - so that you may carry forward the best of your roots, and fly according to your own truest vision. Part One / Side A helps you gather awareness of your roots and your wings *now* in the present, and from the past via your family of origin and lineage. Part Two / Side B provides meditations and guided imagery to strengthen your roots and spread your wings by affirming your spiritual life.

Please do not listen while driving or doing other tasks. However, repeated use of the CD / tape will build inner strength. If strong feelings surface within you, breathe gently to exhale any discomfort, and let the music take you deeper. And if, for any reason, you need to take time out, please put the CD / tape on pause.

Commentary

Your gifts

We are all children of Mother Earth, each a cell of the planet, affecting the health of the whole. Yet like snowflakes, no two of us are alike. Whatever your experience of the past, your family and culture, your unique life is a gift and challenge at this time! As you become more grounded, receiving nourishment from the best of your roots, you will develop the confidence and strength to fly in accordance with your own gifts and vision. When you are happily expressing your own abilities, you are likely to be more joyful and willing to accept others with their cultural differences. Whether small or large, your contribution will effect positive change, adding to co-operation, creativity and peace.

Paradigm shifts

We are living at a pivotal time in history, making the shift from one millenium to another. It isn't so long ago that another pivotal moment of immense significance shifted our perspective on planet earth. That shift came as a result of space travel.

Prior to space travel, we were not truly world inhabitants in the way we are now - *all of us visibly bonded together on one sphere*, part and parcel of the whole. Then, I used to argue that because we had enough poverty and pressing problems on earth, we shouldn't waste money on space exploration. Now, I continue to be amazed by the unforeseen consequences and benefits of the space program and touched by what astronauts have shared.

Space travel has brought significant advances in medical technology as well as new spiritual perspectives. We know that pollution here, or starvation there, is no longer a local problem. Here are some of my favorite quotes from the book *The Home Planet* produced by the Association of Space Explorers. No matter what their nationality or culture, astronauts were in awe of their experience in space:

> *"From Space I saw Earth - indescribably beautiful with the scars of national boundaries gone."* Muhammad Ahmad Faris, Syria.

> *"Before I flew I was already aware of how small and vulnerable our planet is; but only when I saw it from space, in all its ineffable beauty and fragility, did I realize that humankind's most urgent task is to cherish and preserve it for future generations."* Sigmund Jahn, Germany.

> *"Suddenly from behind the rim of the moon, in long, slow-motion moments of immense majesty, there emerges a sparkling blue and white jewel laced with slowly swirling veils of white, rising gradually like a small pearl in a thick black sea of mystery. It takes more than a moment to fully realize this is Earth - home."* Edgar Mitchell, USA.

> *"The first day or so we all pointed to our countries. The third or fourth day we were pointing to our continents. By the fifth day we were aware only of one Earth."* Sultan Bin Salman al-Saud, Kingdom of Saudi Arabia

It takes time to catch up with a paradigm shift. Entering the space age was perhaps the beginning of our preparation for the new millenium. Because this is such a major transition, the preparation will not be complete for several decades still to come. Our challenge is to continue to address, in the twenty-first century, the unresolved issues of community and compassion that will lead to our common good.

This workbook and audio help you move towards the choice of healthy personal responsibility. They encourage you to ask "How can I use my unique gifts to be an agent of transformation on earth, rather than a victim of my circumstances?" and then, they give you tools to find your own answers.

In-depth Insight Page 1

today's date_____

THE INTRODUCTION

WHEN I THINK OF MYSELF AS A CELL OF THE PLANET AND A CHILD OF MOTHER EARTH, I honor my connection to others, and what I have in common with them.

I especially am thankful for . . .

WHEN I THINK OF THE WONDERFUL VARIATIONS IN LIFE AT ALL LEVELS - mineral, plant, animal, human - I celebrate both the universe's diversity and my individuality.

I specifically appreciate . . .

WHEN I LOOK BACK AT MY LIFE, I am aware of important shifts in awareness . .

I recognize this key turning point . . .

It took place when . . .

ROOTS AND WINGS

EXPLORING YOUR ROOTS, DISCOVERING YOUR WINGS

Text of Audio: Track 2

Settle in now, sitting comfortably with your spine straight. Shut your eyes and let the music and the rhythm of your breath take you deeper into your interior space, breathing in and out, relaxing and letting go, as you enter the world of roots and wings where you may experience your own.

ROOTS: Let the chair or floor support you as you begin to see the roots of a tree going deep down into the earth. Become aware that these roots are part of the living earth, and sense or visualize nourishing energy flowing upwards from the earth. Feel what it's like to become these growing roots. As you breathe deeper and deeper, open the soles of your feet so that your roots may extend downward right into Mother Earth. Keep breathing through your roots into the earth, and when you feel deeply connected, draw in the earth energy, bringing it up through your soles to fill your feet, your ankles, your legs, your torso and then your upper body. Be aware of how you feel as you receive earth's energy. Be with yourself, and your feelings, however you are experiencing them. Gradually bring your awareness gently back to the rhythm of your breath, in and out.

WINGS: Sense now that your body is growing wings. As they expand and reach out into the air, let your upper body be at one with your wings, so that you begin to move freely. Feel your wings moving in the air. Sense the lightness and the freedom. Expand this sense of yourself, and allow your energy to move upward and outward, feeling the gracefulness, as you rise! float! soar! Be with yourself and your feelings as you reach out with wings to the cosmos. Now slowly descend, landing gently on the earth.

Commentary

Experiencing your roots and wings

The first exploration or creative process invites you to get in touch with what *roots* mean to you and then with what *wings* mean to you. With the aid of your imagination you will be able to use your senses (sight, sound, smell, taste, touch) to become aware of how you are rooted, and how you can spread your wings. Some people are highly tuned to seeing, others to hearing, and yet others to sensory impressions. Be open to experience your roots and your wings in any combination of these visual, auditory or kinesthetic ways.

Since roots lead to stability and nourishment and wings lead to freedom, the combined metaphor of roots and wings from nature is a powerful reminder of your ability to regenerate and transform. If you find, initially, that you connect more easily with either your roots or your wings, but not with both, just note your natural preference. As you work with the audio and workbook, be open to a new appreciation of the other less familiar energy and you'll soon be enjoying and dancing with both polarities of your roots and wings.

We learn through play

Let go as much as you can of any overly grown-up or logical sense of what to expect. Play with this exploration. Encourage yourself to enter the world of your roots and wings with the freshness and innocence of a child. Your imagination is not hidebound within your body. It loves to take off. However, remember to come back to the awareness of the rhythm of your breath in your body, at the end of each imaginative journey.

In-depth Insight Page 2

ROOTS AND WINGS

EXPLORING MY ROOTS
I experience my roots as . . .   (describe or draw the shape, color, texture, smell . . .)

When I connect with the earth, I feel . . . (both sensation and emotion)

DISCOVERING MY WINGS
I experience my wings as . . .   (describe or draw the shape, color, texture, smell . . .)

When I take off the ground and soar, I feel . . .

DAILY ALIGNMENT -1

GROUNDING AND PREPARING TO FLY

Text of Audio: Track 3

With your new awareness of roots and wings, think of yourself as being part of a total energy system that supports life here with the land energy of Mother Earth and the cosmic energy of Grandfather Sky. Both these powers support your growth and will work together to strengthen you.

GROUNDING: Feel your feet becoming roots planted firmly on the ground. Focus in on your body between your chest and lower abdomen to discover a place that feels like your center. If it helps, put your hand there so you may feel your breath moving in and out. As your breath goes deeper, use it to create an open pathway for earth energy to move up through your roots into your center. As your roots reach down, open yourself more and more to welcome the strength, grounding and comfort of Earth's energy. Draw up as much as you need, letting it permeate every cell in your body.

PREPARING TO FLY: Now welcome the limitless cosmic energy as you take time to expand your breathing to bring in the Spirit of Life. Inhale as much as you comfortably can, and fill your center and then your entire body, letting its lightness permeate every cell.

Commentary

This basic alignment supports your growth as a person. It is a good way to begin each day. It shows you first how to find your center and then how to connect directly to the power and groundedness of the earth and the expansiveness of the universe.

We are supported from beneath and from above

Think of yourself as being part of a total energy system that supports life here. You can, of course, take in nourishment from all around, for example from music or a beautiful sunset. Here you are asked to become familiar with the two main sources of energy: the grounding *land* energy of Mother Earth, and the light expansive *cosmic* energy of the Heavens - of Grandfather Sky. Getting to know these sources of power and working with them by grounding first before expanding, will strengthen you to create or accept change in your life.

Your "felt-body sense"

It is especially important for you to be centered *in* your body as you do each part of this process so that you will experience a "felt body sense". Then you will really know that your feet are planted on the earth like roots and you will really feel your breathing expand as you bring in the Spirit of Life. You can fill yourself - body, mind, emotion and spirit - with abundant life force energy. If you are out of touch with your body, or up in your head, you will just have an idea about being grounded and about preparing to fly. If you are not sure where your center is, let your hands help you to discover it. Move your hands towards your torso, then up and down, letting them alight on the place that feels most like your core or center. Taking time to discover this "felt-body" sense of your core and of support from below and from above will prepare you for whatever the next hour or day will bring.

Cellular exchange
Energy knows no physical barrier or limitation. Invite the balancing energy of earth and sky to permeate right down to the cellular level of your being. You *are* energy, no matter how dense or solid your body appears. Knowing that your body is fluid and constantly changing, (e.g., 98% of the atoms in your body were not there a year ago. Skin cells are renewed every month, and stomach lining cells, every four days) will help you welcome outer change.

Centering and grounding are important prerequisites before you explore your family of origin. It is always wise to center and ground in the present before going back to your past.

In-depth Insight Page 3

DAILY ALIGNMENT -1

THINKING OF MYSELF AS A PART OF A TOTAL ENERGY SYSTEM,
I become aware of . . .

AS I FOCUS ON MY CENTER,
I become aware of . . .

IN PRACTICING THE DAILY ALIGNMENT,
I experience earth's energy as . . .

Taking time to ground brings me this benefit or gift

I experience the cosmic energy as . . .

Taking time to welcome light and expansiveness to my cells brings this benefit or gift

YOUR FAMILY AND LINEAGE

ABOUT YOUR CHILDHOOD ROOTS

Text of Audio: Track 4

Supported in this way from above and below, you have strengthened yourself and are now ready to explore and re-work the effects of your childhood roots. Your family lineage influences you in many subtle ways. Indeed, your family roots may be nourishing or binding you, or causing conflict in your adult life without your knowledge. If you can distinguish between those roots which help you grow and those which hold you back you have a basis upon which to make clearer choices in your life. As a child of the universe, your true home and identity lie within you.

TIME-TRAVELING PROCESS: Settle in comfortably with your feet on the ground, as you prepare to turn the clock back to view your childhood from the safe distance of now. Perhaps you'll remember some old forgotten events or stories you were told, or be in touch with fantasies you might have had about your parents or childhood caregivers. Don't worry about accuracies.

YOUR CHILDHOOD: Imagine that you are entering your childhood home. Move around from room to room, hearing old forgotten sounds and voices, smelling aromas, and noticing how you feel as you go. Perhaps you remember more than one childhood home. Wherever you are, notice what memories emerge. Recall who is there, and what happened. Maybe you remember times with different parents, or caregivers and how each of them expected you to behave. Find the thread of what was really important to you. Breathe in and out as feelings, memories or stories come up.

EARLIEST MEMORIES: And, remembering that you still have your own adult feet planted on the ground here, continue traveling back to be with your earliest memories as a child or infant. Using all of your senses, notice where you are, who is with you and what is happening. Even let yourself recall whatever you know of your birth and how you were welcomed into the world.

YOUR PARENTS or CAREGIVERS: From birth on, you were greatly affected by those who cared for you, and you may have been troubled, hurt or confused by some of their actions. Recognizing how each side of your family has influenced you, may help you understand your story.

MOTHER'S SIDE OF FAMILY: So, as the witnesser, travel again further back through time to separate out some of the strands of your lineage. Let your focus shift to your mother, or the person who was mother to you. Imagine how she looked and how she felt as you picture her as a child. What were the messages she got about being a little girl and growing up? Reflect on how you have been influenced by your mother's background, history and family tales. Recall what you can of your maternal grandparents, their lives, origins and lineage.

FATHER'S SIDE OF FAMILY: Taking another deep breath, gradually turn your attention to your father or the person who was father to you. Picture him in his surroundings as a boy, how he looked and how felt about himself, and what he was taught about life. Reflect on how you have been influenced by your father's background, history and family stories. Recall your paternal grandparents, their lives, origins and lineage.

Commentary

Preparation

This many faceted and many layered exploration can open the door to a multitude of new insights over time. It is particularly useful at this point, before you step out of the present into the past, to refer back to *"How To Use The Audio and Workbook"* on page 5. There you will find practical suggestions such as - work at your own pace and in your own time, turn the audio off when you need to, allow the music to carry you along, and when you make journal entries by writing or drawing, don't try to capture everything at once.

Always include centering and grounding as part of your preparation for this or any process involving memories of your childhood. To anchor yourself firmly in current time, look around your room, so that you are familiar with your surroundings before beginning. Note three favorite belongings or things you like - the flowers in a vase, the color of your carpet, the painting on the wall. This is the place to which you can return at any time. It is important to be in the now as an adult with your two feet planted on the ground. In this way, you will begin to develop the "witnesser", the part of you that can observe and remain grounded at all times.

The influence of your past

Your family, lineage and culture continue to influence you long after you leave your childhood home and neighborhood. Like all children, you have absorbed the "do's and don'ts", and the attitudes of your family, often without even realizing it. Healthy roots encourage strong growth, binding roots weaken and limit growth. You can gain strength now by facing truthfully what is and moving ahead from there.

The purpose of time-traveling

Time traveling, or journeying to your past, enables you to turn the clock back in memory and/or imagination to the years when you were a child, without actually leaving your room. In revisiting your childhood, you will gather information, getting in touch both with what happened to you and how you responded to people and events. You will learn to distinguish between roots that nourished you and roots that bound you. Since history continually rewrites itself, you will gain a new perspective from this moment.

Whatever you discover, I would like to remind you that you are not simply defined as a child of your birth parents or even of adopted parents. You are a child of the Universe, and as such, your true home and identity lie within you. You are no longer beholden to others, no matter how often adults, either blood family members or other caregivers, controlled or made life difficult for you.

Whatever you see or experience when you turn the clock back is *not* happening now, although it may deeply affect you. You may remember half-forgotten memories or intense feelings from time to time. If you begin to feel overwhelmed, place your feet firmly on the ground, become more fully the witness or neutral observer, and breathe deeply. On a count of three, time travel *forward* to where you are now sitting or lying. Connect again with your surroundings, for example the flowers in the vase, the color of the carpet, the painting on the wall, and relax.

Listen to your body sensations when you time-travel

Everything that happens to you is registered in your body. Your body is a storehouse of memories and feelings of all past events. It doesn't lie. Unfortunately, many children have to overlook their own basic feelings in order to be accepted in their family, please their caretakers or avoid punishment. Doing so numbs or masks feelings. If you were such a child, when you time-travel you may be surprised to discover a feeling that you didn't expect. It could be one that was camouflaged or disowned when you didn't know what to do with it earlier. Such emotions can remain hidden inside you for a very long time. Uncovering past likes and dislikes is important. As you go to your past from this moment, trust your capacity to register feelings that surface *now* about what was good for you and what wasn't *then*. For further guidance to help you at those times when you get in touch with strong feelings from the past, please turn to *On Strong Feelings* in *Additional Resources* on page 70.

Feelings are facts

Your subjective feelings about a person or an event must be given as much, if not more, consideration as so-called objective facts. If you get caught up in trying to remember everything accurately, including correct calendar dates etc., your left brain will have a field day, but you may override intuitive impressions that your right brain can provide. Literal accuracy is not the point.

You may never know exactly the difference between what you actually remember about your early years and what you have been told by others or seen in photographs. There is always a blending of fantasy and reality. Especially in the section about your parents, you have no way of differentiating what actually happened from what you were told and what you have deduced yourself.

Selective perception is natural

It doesn't matter if you, your friends and family members all remember things differently. Just as eyewitnesses on the scene of an accident vary greatly in the details they report to the police, so too, each individual has a different vantage point for recalling the past. Relax as you time-travel. You are not in a situation where failing to remember something is a matter of life or death. Nor is it a test you need to pass. Don't worry if you have more than one feeling, some even conflicting. That's perfectly normal. Remain open, alert to receive whatever comes to you, with as little judgment as possible about yourself and others.

The thread of importance

No doubt many activities you enjoyed doing as a child fell by the wayside as you grew up. Choice is inevitable. As you pursued one track at school, you probably had to leave some other interests undeveloped. Such unexplored possibilities are not dead. They are merely dormant and may, like seeds, be waiting for you to nurture them into life again. It is worth re-awakening them.

From one generation to another

Our actions reach far into the future. "The sins of the fathers are visited on the sons to the seventh generation" is part of Judaic teachings. Among native Americans, any tribal decision must take the future into consideration. Is the choice good for the children and the children's children *and* the children's children's children?

Threads of influence can be traced genetically and socially backwards and forwards in time. Ancestors contribute more to the future than is generally realized. Exploring your connection to previous generations can be enlightening, even though your early childhood memories are initially faint. Like many children, you may have received more time and affection from a favorite grandparent than from your own preoccupied parents. Many genetic traits or gifts skip a generation or two before surfacing again. As you work with the material in *Your Family and Lineage*, your memories may stir up unexpected connections - perhaps a feeling for a great-aunt or the recognition of a quality or characteristic that you have inherited. It has been there in the mix all the time, without your conscious recollection.

The more you use this exploration, the easier time-traveling becomes. You will develop the knack of trusting that the memory or fantasy which surfaces each time is the "right" one, without being greedy for more. Other memories will come later. When the spaces on the Family and Lineage pages are not sufficient for all the memories that come flooding in, use them for the highlights, and begin to fill in the details on a My Memories page, using as many extra blank pages as you need.

In-depth Insight Page 4

today's date _____

FAMILY AND LINEAGE

MY CHILDHOOD MEMORIES *(in words, drawing or diagram)*

WHEN I REVISITED MY CHILDHOOD HOME,

This is what I saw

This is what I heard

This is what I smelled

This is what I sensed

This is what I felt

PEOPLE I REMEMBER (parents, siblings and others)

I specifically recall _____

This is how I experienced my connection with him/her . . .

The words or actions I appreciated were . . .

The words or actions I didn't understand were . . .

In-depth Insight Page 5

today's date _____

FAMILY AND LINEAGE *(continued)*

MY CHILDHOOD MEMORIES *(continued)*

INCIDENTS OR FAMILY EVENTS   . . .

THIS WAS REALLY IMPORTANT TO ME AS A CHILD . . .   *(For example, a hobby, a skill, a toy, a friend, a grandparent, a place, or something else)*

My feelings connected with it were . . . (e.g. I loved to, was excited about . . .)

MY EARLIEST MEMORIES ARE ABOUT . . .

I REMEMBER THIS STORY ABOUT MY BIRTH / EARLY CHILDHOOD . . .

In-depth Insight Page 6

FAMILY AND LINEAGE (continued)

MY MOTHER'S SIDE OF THE FAMILY - A COLLAGE / MOSAIC OF IMPRESSIONS

ABOUT MY MOTHER OR THE PERSON WHO WAS MOTHER TO ME . . .

(For example, here you might note the most important influences and people in her life, the events that affected her, her friends, what others have told you about your mother as well as your own experience of her and her relatives.)

THIS STORY ABOUT MY MOTHER'S FAMILY, RELATIVES, LINEAGE, OR ANCESTORS surfaced today . . .

In-depth Insight Page 7

today's date _____

FAMILY AND LINEAGE *(continued)*

MY FATHER'S SIDE OF THE FAMILY - A COLLAGE / MOSAIC OF IMPRESSIONS

ABOUT MY FATHER OR THE PERSON WHO WAS FATHER TO ME . . .
(For example, note the most important influences and people in his life, the events that affected him, his friends, what you have been told about him, as well as your own experience of him. and his relatives)

THIS STORY ABOUT MY FATHER'S FAMILY, RELATIVES, LINEAGE, OR ANCESTORS surfaced today . . .

In-depth Insight Page 8

FAMILY AND LINEAGE (continued)

REVIEW

BEING A MEMBER OF MY FAMILY WHEN I WAS YOUNG WAS LIKE . . .

It brought up these feelings . . .

When I plant my own two adult feet firmly on the ground in this moment,
I RECOGNIZE THAT THE ROOTS THAT HAVE BOUND ME MOST WERE/ ARE . . .
(perhaps family, neighborhood, cultural, national roots?)

AND...THE ROOTS THAT HAVE NOURISHED ME MOST, and from which I still draw
strength, are . . .

BEING A MEMBER OF MY FAMILY NOW IS LIKE . . .

TRANSFORMING YOUR PAST

REFRAMING AND RE-WORKING YOUR FAMILY ROOTS

Text of Audio: Track 5

Sense the rich mixture of genes from both sides of your family and lineage now within you. Through their gift of life to you, even if there has been struggle and pain, *you* have the choice, as a Child of the Universe, to redirect your life, and to weave these strands of the past in a new way.

RELEASING: As you inhale a couple of deep cleansing breaths, fully inhabit yourself. Become aware of some things from your past that haven't helped you, that you don't wish to hold on to. In this moment, exhaling deeply, choose to release something. Whatever it is, let it go, give it a color and send it down through your legs and feet, deep into Mother Earth with the prayer that it be absorbed into the greater Life Force.

BLESSINGS IN DISGUISE: And now remember that, whatever your upbringing, you are unique and you are able to change whatever you have perceived as a limitation. Bring such an experience to the light and look for the gift within. Welcome and integrate this blessing in disguise, re-weaving it into your life.

GIVING THANKS: And, if there's a person, quality, or experience from your family and lineage that you wish to honor, quietly be with them that they may continue to bless your life. Be filled to overflowing, as you breathe in their love, letting it merge with your appreciation and gratitude. Give thanks for all the gifts you have received which open you to love, beauty, health and goodness.

Commentary

You can redirect your life

Your parents have passed on the gift of life to you, blending genes from many, many ancestors. You are more than the sum total of your genes and circumstances. Even if you don't know who your parents are or if you have had a hard life, your past provides the raw material from which you grow and create now. As a child of the Universe you can redirect your life. You are resilient and your capacity to survive is magnificent. You can build on your past and work creatively to extract the positive from the negative in your heritage. This is equally true if you were adopted, have no memories of your grandparents or parents, or have been brought up by other caregivers. Do not think you must know all the factual details of your past to be able to heal or change it. Once you have begun to review your childhood, you can proceed to the next step of re-framing its meaning.

Three tools for transformation

Transforming Your Past provides three tools to help you use the information you have gathered in *Your Family and Lineage*. With them you can reframe the meaning and rework the effects of your childhood roots so that you will experience and reclaim your own power and freedom. The *first* shows you how to release negativity, the *second* suggests how you can look for a gift in what you had previously perceived as a limitation, and the *third* enables you to give thanks for blessings in your life. I have found that these powerful keys open doors towards change.

1. **You must release the past, and especially the negativity from the past,** if you want to live fully in the present. You are no longer the child you were. Although your family's influence may have been moderated by others who introduced new options into your life, old habits die hard. You may be tempted to hold on to your past, sometimes rigidly, just because it is familiar. In *Your Family and Lineage*, you may have connected with old hurts or family habits and assumptions that are not now appropriate to how *you* choose to live. When you hold on to old fears, angers, or justifications, everything in your life begins to solidify and eventually freeze. This, in turn, gives more power to negativity. When you release your past, forgive yourself and others for making mistakes, you generate warmth again.

   Select something specific from your past that you are ready to release, for example, an old grudge or a debilitating belief. Letting go is part and parcel of forgiveness. When you are no longer invested in maintaining your resentment or making another pay for past actions, you are free to be use your energy more creatively. It is better to choose something small that you are really ready to release than go for something big that creates ambivalence in you. Use your breath *and* ride the wave of the music to send it on its way energetically. The metaphor of the earth composting our negativity is very relevant for this exploration.

2. **You can turn a limitation into a blessing.** By looking for a gift in what you have previously perceived as a limitation, you are changing your frame of reference or re-framing. When you extract the good from even a negative heritage you can bring your creativity to bear in any circumstance, not only at favorable times. By turning around one experience at a time, you will increasingly discover and demonstrate that you are not a victim of your past. For example, wounded healers are those who, out of their own pain, have learned to develop great sensitivity and compassion for others.

3. **Saying thank you** is a very simple but often overlooked way of building positive energy. Appreciation works wonders. It builds bridges between you and others and helps you develop trust in yourself. It opens your heart and helps things start moving again when they have been stuck.

Focus on giving thanks for one particular person, event or experience. As you appreciate your gifts and honor the wonder and mystery of other people and the beauty of nature around you, you contribute to the flow of positive energy. Scan your past for blessings, enhance your capacity for gratitude and contribute more light towards happiness, harmony, love and peace on the earth!

By choosing to work with these three tools, you will become more aware of what it means to live according to your highest choice for yourself. Little by little, your inner integrity will be expressed more fully in your outer life. By transforming your past in this way, you will find it easier to develop compassion for yourself and others. It is also likely that you will touch deeper mysteries of life. You will be truly ready to explore your spiritual roots and wings, with a view to co-creating your present and future in a new way - the focus of Part Two.

In-depth Insight Page 9

today's date _____

TRANSFORMING YOUR PAST

MY FAMILY'S LEGACY

SENSING THE RICH MIXTURE OF GENES WITHIN ME, I appreciate the joys, sorrows, struggles and achievements of my forebears, known and unknown.

I specifically honor _____   who . . .

I CALL ON MY ANCESTORS TO BEAR WITNESS, as I redirect my life in this new way . . .
(perhaps following the inspiration of some forebears or walking away from the choices of others)

USING THE THREE TOOLS FOR TRANSFORMATION

1. RELEASING THE PAST
   I call on my courage and resilience, as I release . . .

   I am willing to let it go and recycle it back to the earth to nurture future growth. I . . .

In-depth Insight Page 10

today's date _____

TRANSFORMING YOUR PAST *(continued)*

2. TURNING LIMITATIONS INTO BLESSINGS
   I choose to turn around this old negativity . . .

   I recognize this gift in the "limitation" . . .

3. SAYING THANK YOU
   I open my heart and fill myself with appreciative memories of _____ who has blessed my life in this way . . .

   I choose to express my thanks by . . .   (e.g., you might call, meet, or write the one you remember (if alive); say a prayer; planting a tree. . .)

   I give thanks for these other gifts of love, beauty, health and goodness . . .

BRIEF INTRODUCTION TO PART TWO and to INVOCATION

Text of Audio: Track 6

INTRODUCTION: Part Two provides meditations and guided imagery to help you connect with your spiritual roots and wings, and honor your kinship with all life. So settle in again. Let yourself get quiet to ask for help from the Universe in the form of this Invocation. Follow along with what feels right for you, letting go of what doesn't. It guides you from your external concerns to an inner sacred space, where you honor Great Spirit, or the Divine in your life. It also acknowledges the powers and the gifts that flow to us from all around.

INVOCATION AND BLESSING

HONORING THE DIVINE IN YOUR LIFE

Text of Audio: Track 7

INVOCATION: Center yourself by taking a few deep, cleansing breaths and at the sound of the singing bowls, join with me as you make this invocation your own.

Honor Great Spirit, Creative Source of Light and Life in the Universe. Ask for a blessing from Great Spirit to surround you -

Facing East, honor the Powers of the East and ask for the blessing of clarity and creativity to light up your path.

Facing South, honor the Powers of the South and ask for the blessing of trust and innocence to keep you open.

Facing West, honor the Powers of the West and ask for the blessing of silence to deepen your inward journey.

Facing North, honor the Powers of the North and ask for the blessing of wisdom to guide you.

Welcome any guides, guardians, teachers, protectors in spirit to assist you for your greatest good and release any negativity, which you may send to the Greater Light for healing.

Bend down towards the earth to honor Mother Earth. Look up to the sky to honor Grandfather Sky and go within to honor the Divine within you.

Commentary

Shifting gears

I have put together this invocation and blessing from a number of traditions that are meaningful to me. It prepares you to shift gears by guiding you from the busyness of your daily schedule and your external concerns to a timeless non-linear space. It sets a quiet context for your inner journey as part of the Greater Whole where you can center yourself. By slowing down, you will find you have enough time to do what you need to do, and be who you want to be. Acknowledging the interconnectedness of mind, body, emotions and spirit, you will establish a safe and sacred context for seeds of change to grow in your life. It also affirms that you are a child of the Universe, not only of your birth parents.

The Divine

You may find it useful to review the *Thoughts on Meditation* on page 67 with special reference to naming the Divine. Although I introduce various names for the concept of God, please use the one with which you are most comfortable. If, at some point, you are drawn to use another name, let that be part of the organic growth of your process.

Enlisting help

The invocation honors the Divine and the powers of the seven directions - four traditional ones (North, East, South and West) starting in the East, down (Mother Earth), up (Grandfather Sky), and within (The Divine Life Force within you). Some people like to sit quietly without moving during the Invocation, facing each direction inwardly. Others prefer to stand up and physically turn towards each as it is named. Experiment both ways. I have chosen a few simple attributes traditionally associated with each direction. From time to time, a specific phrase, perhaps about a direction, will catch your attention, while others may not appeal to you. Focus on those that are meaningful, and let go of any words or concepts that are not. Feel free to weave other meanings into your invocation. For example, you may honor Jesus as your Guide, or you may know that east is associated with air and the Archangel Raphael, south with fire and Michael, west with water and Gabriel, and north with earth and Auriel.

Singing bowls

The singing bowls that you hear come from Tibet. They are beautiful bowls, each unique, hand-hammered by monks who created them in Tibetan Buddhist monasteries. Traditionally, metals (gold, silver, copper, iron, lead, tin etc.) were used. Singing bowls create powerful vibrations and harmonic tones when the player strikes or circles the outside rim of the bowl with a leather-covered wooden stick. Allow your cells to be permeated by the sound vibrations and sense how your own individual response to the singing bowls varies at different times.

In-depth Insight Page 11

INVOCATION AND BLESSING

GREAT SPIRIT IN MY LIFE
I was brought up to think of Great Spirit or God as . . .

My sense of God now is . . .

My name for the Divine is . . .

SHIFTING GEARS
As I center myself with the Invocation, I experience . . .

The words which most touch and resonate within me are . . .

The direction that resonates within me most is . . .

In-depth Insight Page 12

today's date _____

INVOCATION AND BLESSING *(continued)*

ENLISTING HELP
I welcome this presence / these presences (perhaps a guide or guardian, or more than one Spiritual Being), even if my awareness is just for a brief moment, . . .

I specifically ask for help to . . .

With help, I release this negativity to the Greater Light for healing . . .

When I allow myself to get in touch with my inner divinity, I . . .

SINGING BOWLS
The sound of the singing bowls reaches deep into my . . . (perhaps a part of your body, your mind, emotions or spirit)

DAILY ALIGNMENT – 2

CONNECTING EARTH AND HEAVEN

Text of Audio: Track 8

Deepen your centering by feeling the rhythm of your breath. Connect to your center, and bring the breath down through your legs, through your feet into Mother Earth. Sense your roots going deep into the earth, and find a place - a rock, crystal, or log where you may connect your roots. When you feel stable and well grounded, begin to bring up the energy of the earth. Feel earth's comfort, calm and strength flowing into your feet first, then your legs, all the muscles and organs of your pelvis, and up to your center. After you feel full there, continue to bring it to the upper half of your body - your arms, your throat and your head - so that all of you is filled with the nurturance you need.

Bring your attention to your breath again. Feel your rib cage expand with each breath as you now inhale the lightness and expansion of the Spirit of Life that balances the groundedness. Bring it down to your lower belly and to your feet to ground it through your soles.

Commentary

Every day is a good day to center and ground
This is another version of the basic alignment introduced in Part One. It assumes that you are already aware of and know how to make a connection with your center. It asks you to send your roots down to a specific place that feels good to you, such as a rock deep in the earth where you may anchor and receive nourishment. You will learn to track the flow of energy throughout your body from your toes to your crown. It also assumes that you are in touch with your breathing pattern and encourages you to use your breath for lightness and expansion.

The importance of centering and grounding cannot be overemphasized as the basis of your inner spiritual work as well as your outer work. Using this variation will reinforce your earlier experience.

In-depth Insight Page 13

today's date _____

DAILY ALIGNMENT - 2

BEFORE CENTERING WITH THE DAILY ALIGNMENT,
I felt...

WHILE DEEPENING MY CENTERING WITH THE DAILY ALIGNMENT,
This part of me seemed filled . . .

This part of me felt depleted and needed extra nurturing . . .

This part of my body felt open and light . . .

This part of my body felt compacted and heavy . . .

AFTER CENTERING,
I noticed or felt . . .   *(perhaps a shift or change in your thoughts, body, feelings, spirit, etc.)*

FOR OPTIMAL BALANCE,
I choose to pay more attention to . . .

BEING IN THIS MOMENT

ATTENDING TO YOUR INNER EXPERIENCE

Text of Audio: Track 9

> Continue to go within, sensing what is happening in this moment. Just *be* exactly where you are. As you become quiet, a feeling may rise to the surface, or a sensation in part of your body, or a memory or an image. . . Let yourself be with your inner experience in a friendly yet detached way without praise or blame. Linger. Listen to yourself or any part of your body that claims your attention and welcome any message that comes to you from deep within.

Commentary

The principle of homeostasis
This principle, at work within everyone, seeks to keep you in a healthy balance by giving you early warning signals when you get *out* of balance. If you pay close attention to your body's signals, such as an ache, a pain or exhaustion, you will learn what you may have neglected or over-used. When you cooperate, for example, by slowing down after pushing yourself too hard, you'll renew and rebalance yourself as you journey through each phase of your life. It is equally important to pay attention to your feelings so that you also know what makes you really happy or contented. Take a moment to identify how your own early warning signals get your attention.

Be as open as possible
No praise, no blame is an attitude of open attention, or open inquiry, where you put the filter of your judging mind aside. The judging mind makes things good or bad, right or wrong, according to a set of beliefs or dogma it has been trained to adhere to. It is therefore not able to be truly open to the present moment with its clues, messages and subtle nuances from sensations, fleeting memories, images or feelings.

As you become more available, present and receptive in the moment, you can honor a wide range of feelings, whatever they are. You may experience more than one feeling, even contradictory ones, at the same time, as you did when you were time-traveling. Memories and their associated feelings are often held in different parts of your body and they may surface almost simultaneously.

In-depth Insight Page 14

today's date _____

BEING IN THIS MOMENT

WHEN I LISTEN DEEPLY AND TRACK MY INNER EXPERIENCE,
I am aware of the following...

      emotions

      sensations

      memories

      images

      colors

      sounds

THIS PART OF MY BODY CLAIMS MY ATTENTION
I sense it wants me to know . . .

AS I LEARN TO BE MORE FRIENDLY TO MYSELF,
I release this judgment or debilitating belief . . .

THE ROOTED ONE'S GROWTH & THE WINGED ONE'S FLIGHT

GUIDANCE FOR YOUR JOURNEY

Text of Audio: Track 10

As your inner journey unfolds, allow any tension you have become aware of to melt away, knowing that you are supported where your sit or lie.

YOUR GROWTH UNTIL NOW: See yourself as a seed or a bulb being planted. Look around and feel where you are. As your roots begin to take hold, be aware of the earth, its texture, its smell. See what you see, feel what you feel, as your roots grow under the surface and connect with your nourishment. When you are ready to emerge from the earth, push up through the soil to the light, look around at what is out there above the ground. Be aware of your own becoming and how you are growing in your early days.

The seasons turn, and you experience in yourself times of unfolding, blossoming, and fruitfulness, times of letting go, hibernation, and times of death and rebirth. The seasons continue to turn until you become aware of yourself fully grown. Notice what's happening to you now, what season it is and what surrounds you. Become aware of how you feel about yourself and this cycle of your life.

ASKING FOR GUIDANCE: Know that you may ask for guidance about your life and what's needed for your growth. Feel your longing for a friendly winged one, a messenger of the Divine, to fly to you to share wisdom and encouragement and to give you an overview, a different perspective. As you send a prayer asking to connect with such a being, you remember - that *you* have the capacity become a messenger of the Divine!

Breathe deeply into the place behind your heart, where your wings may emerge, and with each breath feel your wings taking form and unfolding with wonder and magic. Experiencing your upper body and your wings as one, reach out with strength and grace as the winged being you already are. Sense yourself lifting off the ground, rising with lightness and freedom into the currents of air, ascending, up, up, circling around, getting a different perspective on all that is growing down below on the earth. As you look down, you recognize the rooted one who has called you forth. You know beyond a shadow of a doubt that the rooted one below also recognizes you, and with anticipation is waiting for you to descend.

As you now connect on the earth, the bond of kinship between you grows stronger, creating a safe magical circle of love, a sacred space for both of you to share wisdom, guidance and love. Send your words of wisdom on wings of love right down to the core of the rooted one. Feel the joy and acceptance as the rooted one welcomes your guidance.

And you, the witnesser, with your feet planted on the ground and your wings reaching to the heavens, know in your heart that you are both the rooted one and the winged one, and you are inter-connected. Know, with complete confidence, that this sharing is for your highest good. Allow it to nourish you.

Commentary

Your growth until now

Within one lifetime, each person goes through many cycles. You may sense that you are at the beginning, the middle or the end of a cycle, or in a dormant period before new growth. Each phase is essential to your growth. Like the life-cycle of a plant in which the new season's budding leads to blossoms, flowers, fruit and eventually to the falling of leaves, you too experience the rhythm of birth, growth, death and rebirth. You may have personal preferences about a specific season, but you cannot make it last forever. Your inner seasons don't necessarily correspond to the seasons in the year, although you will often find it helpful to align your activities to the outer seasons. For example, withdrawing into hibernation is most appropriate in winter. This part of the exploration enables you to tune in intuitively to your growth as a *Rooted One*.

Asking for guidance

"Ask and you shall receive" is a teaching that many of us fail to implement on our own behalf, if we have been taught to put others first and not be selfish. Yet asking for help for ourselves can come from a deep sense of trust and inter-relatedness, not just from greed or pain. The willingness to show your ignorance or limitation invites cooperation from the Divine. Asking from a place of trust and open inquiry always leads to the possibility of greater wisdom. Socrates was said to be wise because he acknowledged that he didn't know. Take heart! Your prayers may be answered in gradual, sudden or unexpected ways.

Your Higher Self

This section of the exploration is a parable or story that metaphorically enables you to call on another aspect of yourself, not always honored in our culture - that part of you connected to your inner divinity. Sometimes called the Higher Self or Transpersonal Self, it is wise, knowing and unperturbed by difficulties, always remaining connected to Source. It is variously experienced as a guiding presence, a still small voice or a spark of divinity within. It is different from your every day personality. It is also different from your conscience since your conscience is a reflection of moral teachings you have received from family and culture.

Your Higher Self, the Winged One, is that aspect of yourself that remains clear, no matter what happens in your life. It will not force you to listen, but it is always there. Its voice is akin to that of your true self, reminding you of your union with the Creator and of truth, love, compassion and other transpersonal qualities of which you are capable. It also assists you with your life-task - that which you came here to do or learn.

The Rooted One's Growth and The Winged One's Flight reminds you that you need not go outside of yourself for guidance. "God" or the Divine speaks through *and* within you. Your bond of kinship provides the circle of love and safety, a sacred space for sharing.

Take time to linger whenever you can at the end of this exploration.

In-depth Insight Page 15

today's date _____

THE ROOTED ONE'S GROWTH & THE WINGED ONE'S FLIGHT

THE ROOTED ONE

PAST GROWTH
I received this image or sense about my early growth . . . (perhaps a plant, flower, tree or something else)
I was a . . .

As I grew, new impressions of my growth came to me . . .

CURRENT GROWTH AND SEASON
I am currently experiencing the season of . . .

I'm a . . .

Facing this challenge . . .

MY HEART'S LONGING AND PRAYER IS . . .

In-depth Insight Page 16

today's date _____

THE ROOTED ONE'S GROWTH & THE WINGED ONE'S FLIGHT
(continued)

THE WINGED ONE

AS I RECOGNIZE MY CAPACITY TO BECOME A MESSENGER OF THE DIVINE,
my heart feels . . .

As I breathe deeply into the place behind my heart where my wings can emerge, and rise up, I sense . . .

THE BOND OF KINSHIP

WHEN THE ROOTED ONE AND THE WINGED ONE RECOGNIZE EACH OTHER, AND THEN CONNECT WITHIN ME,
this is what I feel and experience . . .

THE WINGED ONE'S HEARTFELT WORDS OF WISDOM, LOVE AND GUIDANCE
for the rooted one are . . .

THIS EXCHANGE GIVES ME MORE TRUST AND CONFIDENCE TO . . .

THE UNIVERSE'S ABUNDANT GIFTS

WELCOMING BLESSINGS LARGE AND SMALL

Text of audio: Track 11

Since the universe is abundant and generous in response to whatever you ask from deep within you may continue to be nourished from many sources as you grow and transform on your path.

SAFE PLACE: Let yourself go to a place that feels very safe and nourishing. It may be familiar or unfamiliar, perhaps a place outdoors in nature that you have visited, or a building that holds power for you. Or it may be an imagined place which has just the right sense of balance or awe or peace. Wherever it is, let it nurture you now, healing your past and energizing your hopes and dreams.

OTHER BLESSINGS: As you linger there in your special place, remember other blessings which have given your life meaning - perhaps an experience of mystery, or a time of synchronicity, a coincidence, or a moment of deep loving or prayer when you were open to the wonder of life. Let these fill you now.

Commentary

Past blessings continue to nurture you
This exploration reminds you that the universe is abundant. Because we live in such a negative culture it is likely that you have absorbed a negative perspective from those around you. Several studies show that in primary school years, "no" and "don't" are repeated to children far more frequently than "yes" and "you can". I invite you to change your focus by looking beyond limitations or lacks in your past to find nourishment. Even the smallest blessing can support you. Since your perspective influences what you allow into your life, this first step will shape your world in a new way. Be generous to yourself with your memories of blessings. Little blessings are as important as big ones.

The benefits of a safe space
The second step is to visit a place that is safe and nourishing for you, one that you already know, or a new place, created through active imagination, that supports your journey today. Here you will be able to relax more deeply into a sense of safety. The safer you become, the easier it will be for you to trust yourself and your own process and *not* just what others say you *should* trust. Being in your own safe space will also help you to reconnect to that deeper part of you - your Higher Self.

"Whatsoever is true, whatsoever is beautiful, think on these things . . ."

The third step gives you time to focus on whatever you want to expand in your life. Just as carrying burdens from the past pulls you down energetically, so dwelling on past hurts and other people's shortcomings does not make your life happier or easier. If you constantly harbor critical thoughts, you will notice failings and failures all around you, and it is likely you will have little appreciation or generosity of spirit towards yourself and others.

On the other hand, if you recognize daily blessings in your life - an act of kindness here, a word of encouragement there - you will nurture happiness and a sense of wellbeing and will be able to extend that to others. Look for beauty and you will find it. As you awaken your sense of wonder, remember those times in the past when the earth showed her beauty to you. Remember times when your own beauty shone through.

You will see what you look for
Whatever you feed in your life grows larger, while whatever you neglect or starve grows smaller. A glass filled to the halfway mark can be described as ½ full or ½ empty. One description gives a feeling of plenty, the other a feeling of lack. *The Universe's Abundant Gifts* helps you awaken to all the good in your life, and that, in turn, will open your heart. Then you may experience more frequently the wonders of life.

If it is difficult for you to recognize blessings, make a list of qualities which, when you experience them, help you to feel happy, contented or expansive. Then when you next do the exploration, you may more easily call to mind a small exchange or happening in which you or others have expressed one of those qualities. Or give yourself permission to do something you really enjoy, but rarely find time for. Remind yourself that being able to do what you love is indeed a blessing.

In-depth Insight Page 17

today's date _____

THE UNIVERSE'S ABUNDANT GIFTS

SAFE SPACE
My safe nourishing space is ...

There I heal these hurts ...

There I energize these dreams ...

I GIVE HEARTFELT THANKS FOR MEMORIES OF ...
Synchronistic happenings and coincidences

The mystery and wonder of life unfolding

Special times of prayer and/or deep loving

Other blessings that have renewed and nourished me
   (e.g., people and animals in your life, books, films, art, creative projects, your gifts and abilities)

BIRTHING YOUR DREAMS

CO-CREATING FOR THE GOOD OF ALL

Text of audio: Track 12

Become aware of your hopes, dreams and wishes lying dormant within you. Be with yourself and your dreams. As you listen to them, feel life stirring within them and sense one rising up from your depth. Welcome and accept it. Trust yourself with it more and more. And knowing that this dream is part of the creativity of the Universe bubbling up through you, recognize with a smile of contentment that you are a co-creator. Affirm your intention and willingness to birth this opportunity. Drawing whatever you need from the Universe, feel your confidence rising as you see your dream unfold.

Honor your connection to the web of life and love, and give wings to your prayer that this unfolding be for the good of all.

CONCLUDING BLESSING: *May you continue to call on these many sources of Inner Light! May they give you added courage to fly! And may your union with the Divine uphold you!*

Commentary

Your hopes, dreams and wishes are important
The daydreaming or dreamlike imagination of a child can lead to purposeful actions later on. Yet you may have been brainwashed into thinking that daydreaming is a waste of time and your imagination unconnected to reality. Not so! In *Birthing Your Dreams*, you are first asked to be attentive to your inner hopes, dreams and wishes, trusting that they will unfold, as you own your part in the creative process. You are a co-creator in the magnificent ongoing creation and dance of life.

Clear intention is a major catalyst for change and transformation
Intention brings strength, energy and focussed spiritual power. When you engage your will to focus your intention on your desired outcome, be as specific as possible. Ask what you need from the Universe for support, becoming fully present and willing to birth the opportunity in front of you. When you are aligned with your Higher Self you are part of the whole web of light and love, in tune with your deepest spiritual purpose.

Now is *not* the time to feed your doubts! When you bring something new into form, or manifest, you may have to suspend old narrow definitions of reality that you were taught in the past. By realizing that the world is *energy*, fluid and moving, not fixed and rigid, you can rethink anything you have been told is either possible or impossible. At the level of energy and atoms, nothing is impossible. Even a fixture like the Berlin Wall can come down. Life is no longer cast in concrete, and you can begin to influence events to release the highest and best potential in every situation.

Your true Self is the most essential core of your Being, and is unique to you. Your dreams, hopes and visions will be unlike any one else's. They deserve your time and attention. Consider taking 10 or 20 minutes a day to focus on your dream. Later you may extend this time. It's better to start in a small way and continue consistently rather than to start with a bang and fizzle out after a week or so.

Manifesting for the good of all

"For the good of all, according to free will, so must it be" are the concluding words of an ancient prayer for manifestation. They set a clear honorable context, which overrides any less worthy goals. When you are in harmony with your own highest good, you connect to transpersonal qualities and values that do not harm others. What you wish for does not then manipulate, force or control others at their expense. As your hopes, dreams and visions bubble up from your depth, sense those that are truly of your essence, uniquely yours, and ask that they may take form in the physical universe for the good of all, in keeping with the spiritual laws of the Universe.

My prayer is that this audio and workbook will be a blessing to you, the listener and reader, on your journey from your roots to your wings. May it reach those whom it will benefit and may it be used for the good of all, according to free will.

In-depth Insight Page 18

BIRTHING YOUR DREAMS

MY DORMANT HOPES, DREAMS AND WISHES
This buried dream bubbled up to the surface from my depths . . .

I welcome it, and am willing to participate fully in its creation, by . . .

I see my vision unfold in this way . . .

I can take one or more of the following steps to help it grow . . .
  - Focus on it in prayer and meditation, asking for help from the Universe that the outcome
  will be for the highest good of all.
  - Share it with trusted friends.
  - Ask for the involvement of others at certain times.
  - Act according to my inner guidance in this way.

The first step I intend to take is . . .

Other steps . . .

MY PRAYER OF BLESSING

  For others

  For myself

In-depth Insight Page 19

today's date _____

AND NOW... WHERE DO I GO FROM HERE?

WHEN IT'S TIME TO REVIEW

On any journey, there are times when it is helpful to review where you've come from before you proceed. When you have completed one cycle of this workbook, and are at a new point in the spiral of your life, consider implementing some of these suggestions to carry you forward.

- *BROWSE through the pages you have written or creatively filled and take time to reflect on all you have accomplished thus far in your workbook. Congratulate yourself.*

- *GO TO THE NEXT PAGE OR TAKE SOME BLANK PAGES - Journal more, write a story, create a poem, paint or draw a picture, offer a prayer . . .*

- *ASK YOURSELF*
  Where am I now?

  Have my feelings changed? If so, how?

  Has my thinking changed? If so, how?

  Do I sense anything different in my body? If so, what?

  Has my relationship to Spirit, or to what I call God or Divine, shifted? If so, how?

  OR

  What feels finished and put to rest?

  What feels unfinished?

  What explorations would I like to take further?

  What inner guidance have I received that I have yet to act on?

  Where do I want to be, one day from now, one week or one year from now?

PUT YOUR JOURNAL ASIDE. Take a deep breath - create a dance - go outside - scream from the top of your lungs - feel the sun/ wind/ snow/ rain. Tune in to your intuition, ask for guidance, wait for your answer and . . .   BON VOYAGE!

In-depth Insight Page 20

today's date _____

AND NOW... WHERE DO I GO FROM HERE? *(continued)*

Journal more, write a story, create a poem, paint or draw a picture, offer a prayer, respond to the questions on the previous page . . .

ADDITIONAL RESOURCES

THOUGHTS TO HELP YOU ON YOUR JOURNEY:

ON RELAXATION

Relaxation feels good, and is good for you

When we relax, we are able to let go of tensions and return to a more natural state in which we become easy and loose, rather than uptight and goal-oriented.

Relaxation is good for your body. It reduces muscle tensions and cramps, lowers your heart rate and blood pressure and helps to recharge and balance your physical energy.

Relaxation is good for your mind. It enhances the functioning of your brain and nervous system and improves the quality of your thoughts and images.

Relaxation is good for your emotions. As you become more centered, it is easier to let go of worry, and release extreme, disturbing or painful feelings.

Relaxation is good for your spirit. It gives you more time to breathe and be inspired by the wonders of life. This can uplift your spirit, allowing it to soar.

Music and voice can assist relaxation

While you are listening, allow the special vibration of the music and the rhythm of my voice to create an inner peace. Music can carry you into a deeply relaxed state of body, mind, emotions and spirit, enabling you to follow along with the explorations or creative processes more easily.

Working with your breath

Throughout the audio, you will be asked to focus on your breath. When you make a slight change, such as deepening or slowing your breath, you change your entire energy field towards greater calm.

While we often take our breathing for granted, awareness of the breath is perhaps the most frequently used method of relaxing, and a most ancient meditative practice. Take, for example, counting the breath. This practice has been used to clear the mind and silence thoughts. Focusing only on one thing at a time, namely the count of your breath, you can go beyond the chattering mind. In a similar fashion, the breathing suggestions in the audio are intended to deepen your relaxation, so that you will be more receptive to your inner journey in the present moment.

ON GUIDED IMAGERY

The benefits of guided imagery

Sometimes known as creative visualization, guided imagery engages the power of your imagination, through the use of selected images, to focus very specifically and purposefully towards a chosen goal. You can use it to increase health, develop a new skill, experience a specific feeling, deepen your relaxation and bring balance to your body, mind, emotions and spirit. In this, guided imagery differs from day dreaming which has no external frame of reference. (Day dreaming allows you to wander freely with your imagination, conjuring up anything, anywhere, any time - past, present, future, but without focus.)

Guided imagery is a very empowering tool

It works best when you are willing to let yourself relax, away from external demands, in a place without hurry and pressure. It's always better to ease gently into imagery rather than grab or force it. If you surrender to the guidance of the words and music, you will be able to go to a deeply relaxed, more diffuse state, where your psyche will provide you with your own images of what is being suggested. For example, if in the exploration where you are asked to "be" in a safe space, you love the ocean and you imagine you are taking it easy on the beach with the sound of the surf in your ears, your body actually will become more peaceful and refreshed.

Sensory imagery

With sensory imagery, you are encouraged to use *all* of your senses: hearing, smelling, touching, even tasting because getting a whole-body sense of what you are imagining has been found to be most effective. In other words, in the example of the beach, you would also *feel* the sun on your skin, *hear* the rhythmic sound of the surf, and even *taste* the salt spray. In fact, many research studies show that when you are relaxed experiencing this whole-body sense, visualization has an even more powerful effect on your life. Imagery can reduce high blood pressure or boost the immune system. Olympic athletes who combined a high proportion of visualization with their physical training showed a measurable increase in their performance.

Imagery on the audio

I have chosen to use guided imagery because it assists you to make valuable changes in your life. First, along with the music, it enables you to relax. Then, in Part One, I encourage you to find your own pictures of roots and wings which you can use in your daily alignment to increase your awareness of grounding and centering. Once grounded, you'll be able to go back to review, reframe, rework and recreate your past. Using imagery in Part Two helps you to take wing as you develop your spiritual life and become light enough to fly in the direction of your choice.

ON MEDITATION

The Divine
In every human there is something that we speak of as Divine. Meditation, contemplation and prayer enable you to reach beyond yourself, or deeply into yourself, to become aware of your connection to your sense of divinity. The Divine is known by many names in different traditions and countries - God, Goddess, Yahweh, Allah, Great Spirit, Universal Love, Essence of Light and Life, Creative Spark in the Universe, the Numinous, Ultimate Reality, "I am that I am", Father, Mother, the Christ Presence etc.

The benefits of connecting with the Divine
When you welcome Divine Power into your life, you will begin to experience that you are not alone. You are a cell of the Universe, part of the Greater Whole of creation. It is the experience of many people that, contrary to their expectations, when they reach "out" to God, they are not going away from themselves but returning more deeply to their own core or essence.

According to William Penn of Pennsylvania, "True worship is to mind and spirit, what sleep is to the body, - nourishment and refreshment". Scientific studies, described by Dr. Larry Dossey and others, now also indicate that prayer and meditation have a very positive affect. They can reduce high blood pressure, heal wounds in humans and increase the germination of seeds in plants. The meditations I offer can act as a catalyst for healing and increased wellbeing as you open yourself directly to Divine Power.

Enlisting help
People of many traditions call on aspects of God, such as the powers of the four directions (North, East, South and West) or the four elements (Earth, Air, Fire and Water), for support. Or they ask messengers of God (Jesus, angels, guardians or saints) to intercede on their behalf as they invoke the power of prayer. You can experience your capacity to call on the Divine and on aspects of God in *The Invocation and Blessing* at the beginning of Part Two.

Silence
Silence is an important part of meditation and prayer. Silence, of course, may be experienced in many ways, depending on the energy it holds or the person from whom it emanates. For example, there are calming silences and threatening silences. Silence in meditation enables you to turn inwards and "practice the presence of God", as the Quakers do. You can choose to experience a silence of open expectation and waiting - where you are receptive and responsive to the Spirit, since God is always waiting to give more than you know to ask. Or perhaps you will choose to be in a silence of focused attention where you continue to fill your mind, quietly and deliberately, with thoughts of God *or* the highest good that you know, e.g. truth, beauty, love. Thus you will become more closely attuned to whatever that highest good is.

If being silent in this way is new to you, I suggest that you experiment from time to time by turning off the audio and waiting in silence, inviting the Spirit of Life. Especially good times to do this would be after *The Invocation*, after listening to both *The Invocation* and *Being in the Now*, or at the end of each half of the audio. Just continue to sit or lie quietly and become receptive to the Unknown.

ON MUSIC

The benefits of music
It goes without saying that music affects people at a very deep level. This is true both for the outdoor music of nature, such as birdsong or crickets, and for music played on musical instruments. Music's language is universal. It can shift your mood in an instant, inspiring you to march or sing or dance to the rhythm of a beat. It can conjure up happy memories and move you to tears.

The Waltz, for example, opens your heart. Studies have shown that listening to Mozart is of great benefit to sufferers from depression. Some music, such as baroque, stimulates your capacity to concentrate and retain the knowledge of what you have been reading. Classical music even increases the growth of plants and the milk-yield of cows!

The music for *ROOTS & WINGS*
Since the frequency and vibration of music can produce such specific results, the choice of music was of prime importance to me. It had to be created in harmony with the sound, rhythm and vibration of my voice in order to express the essence of my work. I asked Richard Shulman, a gifted musician, to use his intuition, first to attune himself to the concept and intention of my words and then to create music to convey and amplify these vibrations and frequencies.

Here are Richard Shulman's recollections of the co-operative venture of creating ROOTS & WINGS:

"When Puja first approached me about creating music for a project to be called *ROOTS & WINGS*, we had a few meetings in which she shared the nature of her work and her vision for the tape[*]. I gave her several options of how we might work together, and she chose my favorite way to co-create such an album, that of recording both the voice track and the music "live" in the studio. I love creating in settings that encourage serendipity, and we were both excited about what we might produce together. We are both indebted to Scott Petito, our engineer who handled the technical details with such skill and ease that Puja and I could concentrate on the creative process.

My job, as I saw it, was to sense the feeling and goal of each piece through listening to Puja and, by connecting with my own Higher Self, to find music that would resonate with the piece. Throughout the session, I asked for music *"for the Highest Good"* for each meditation. The color and vibration of Puja's speaking added inspiration to my creative

---

[*]The *ROOTS & WINGS* audio-tape was created and released in 1996, the CD and workbook in 1999.

process, and the music being created in the moment served to amplify Puja's message. Both the music and the words flowed from our mutual openness to Spirit in such a way that our contributions energized each other as well as the whole."

ON JOURNALING

Writing from your heart

Your hands symbolize your action in life. Extending out from your heart, the act of writing freehand about what is happening within and around you can be profoundly significant. You may well discover that you are expressing much more than you expected to, surprising even yourself. As your head, heart and hand cooperate, you can absorb and understand events in your life afresh. Writing in a journal gives you time for reflection. When you ponder what you have written, those of you who are caught up in busyness can become human *beings* again, rather than human doings.

The benefits of focused journal writing

Free, uncensored, unfocused, or stream of consciousness writing in a diary or journal has been found to reduce stress. Frequently, though, such writing does not bring insight, as the writer tends to cycle around the same issues over and over again. Much more can be achieved through focused or structured journal writing. It can help you take steps to break old patterns and move ahead in your life with new understandings and choices. The *ROOTS & WINGS* exploration pages are set up in this way to give you focused support for transformation.

Communicating to and from your inner self

The *Day-to-Day* journal pages supply you with a number of suggestions which, like warming up exercises at the gym, are intended to loosen you up and get you going. As you respond to them, you will develop the knack of communicating - from and to your inner self. At times you may find yourself writing one or two words or completing a brief sentence. At other times you may write or draw quickly and furiously because you can hardly keep up with thoughts that are tumbling out. As you respond in your own way, you will embark on a rich inward journey where the person you get to know is *you*. Simultaneously, you will be building a foundation to support you from beneath and gaining an overview, a new perspective from above. For future reference it is important to note the date each time you write.

Your own choices

Because *ROOTS & WINGS* is many-layered, it creates a rich texture for you to experience. You may want to listen and respond to some portions more frequently or more fully than others, as first one, then another, important theme comes to the foreground for your attention. Designed to trigger new awareness, the *In-depth Insight* pages will give you support and encouragement to be in a place of open inquiry on your personal journey, section by section. In making your own choices, according to your own inner rhythm, you will be able to gain further insight without trying to do it all at once.

The importance of privacy

What you express is not intended for other eyes. In fact, if you make a pact with yourself that you are writing for you and you alone, then you can really be honest. Keep your journal or workbook in a safe space, out of harm or temptation's reach. (A journal left around might be just too inviting.) Privacy and shelter are important elements for the gestation of seeds growing within your psyche. Your transformation pages can provide comfort, companionship, inspiration and challenge, whatever the phase of your growth.

ON STRONG FEELINGS

It is natural to experience strong feelings from time to time

When you evoke memories of the past, as in *Your Family and Lineage,* you also evoke a feeling response. Please be aware that, although disconcerting, it may now be very good for you to bring hurtful feelings to the light of day, to be addressed and healed, even if you thought you had previously put them to rest or out of your consciousness.

Initially breathe gently to exhale any discomfort

Let the music take you deeper. Sometimes it is simply enough to let the music carry you along. When you ride the wave of the music and soften around the feeling, you will generally find yourself able to stay with the process.

Take time out to love and support yourself

We all have times when we need to acknowledge and release our feelings. Here are some things you can do to love and support yourself if you experience discomfort as strong feelings emerge while you are listening.

- When feelings from the past surface, sense your feet firmly connected to the ground and look around at your familiar surroundings. Deepen and soften your breathing, as you remind yourself that whatever happened to you as a child is *not* happening to you now.

- Put your hand on your belly for comfort, or give yourself a hug.

- Give your feeling a color and drain it out of your body by sending it down your legs into the ground to be absorbed and transformed by the earth. The earth is good at taking negativity (garbage which would make us sick) and turning it into compost for future healthy growth.

- Take the feelings you have stored inside your body, such as annoyance, irritation or anger, and send them to the outside by shaking them from your fingers, arms, and legs. This can also improve the health of your joints where old "stuff" gets stuck.

- Take a shower and, as you clean your skin, ask the water to cleanse and purify your feelings. Let any tears of sadness flow with the water.

- Choose appropriate colors or shapes to draw your feelings.

- Reach out to a friend.

- Shut your eyes, focus on the music, not on the words, and let the music nourish you and lead you into deeper comfort or greater relaxation.

And

- Connect with a therapist or counselor. This audio and workbook have been created primarily for those of you who can benefit from a supportive format for independent in-depth, ongoing work for personal transformation. You can use it in conjunction with other emotional or spiritual inner work. However, it is *not* a substitute for therapy or counseling where the therapeutic relationship is itself a necessary part of the process.

TO SUM UP

With practice, you will become confident using these tools
Meditation, contemplation and prayer have much in common with guided imagery and creative visualization. Each requires a willingness to be in a receptive state in which the muscles of your body are relaxed and your mind becomes still and open. They are also skills that you can train yourself to use. You will find yourself becoming more proficient at these skills as you work with the audio. Relaxation and visualization can pave the way for spiritual awareness, while spiritual connection can further pave the way for true health and wellbeing. Your willingness to journey inwards from the periphery, even through strong feelings, to your essential core will be enhanced by the music and by journal responses written from your heart.

"Only when something is rooted in the earth can it grow into the sky. A tree, to go high in the sky, to whisper to the winds, to dance with the sun, to have a dialogue with the stars, needs first to go deep into the earth, has to spread its roots to the deepest layers of the earth. . ." Osho

OTHER INFORMATION:

BOOKS

RELAXATION, VISUALIZATION

Creative Visualization	Shakti Gawain
Staying Well with Guided Imagery	Belleruth Naparstek
The Relaxation Response	Herbert Benson, M.D.

MUSIC AND MEDITATION

How to Meditate	Lawrence Le Shan
Meditation -The First & Last Freedom (& other titles)	Osho
Music and Miracles (& other titles)	Don Campbell
Singing Bowls	Eva Rudy Jansen
The New Three Minute Meditator	David Harp with Nina Feldman

WRITING/JOURNALING

At a Journal Workshop	Ira Progoff
The Artist's Way	Julia Cameron with Mark Bryan
Writing down the Bones: Freeing the writer within	Natalie Goldberg
Writing from the Body	John Lee

THE FAMILY

Healing the Inner Child	Charlie Whitfield
Homecoming: Championing your inner child	John Bradshaw
Sacred Legacies	Denise Linn
Toxic Parents	Susan Forward

THE EARTH

Earth Prayers	Elizabeth Roberts and Elias Amiden
Healing the Wounds	Judith Plant (Ed.)
Mother Earth Spirituality	Ed McGaa, Eagle Man
The Findhorn Garden	The Findhorn Community
The Home Planet	Kevin W. Kelly (Ed.)

SELF, TRANSFORMATION AND HEALING

Anam Cara - A Book of Celtic Wisdom	John O'Donohue
Healing Words	Larry Dossey, M.D.
Markings	Dag Hammarskjold
On Becoming a Person	Carl Rogers
The Dragon doesn't Live Here Any More, (& other titles)	Alan Cohen
The Road Less Travelled	Scott Peck
The Wheel of Life	Elisabeth Kubler-Ross. MD
Towards a Psychology of Being	Abraham Maslow
Tuesdays with Morrie	Mitch Albom
Wheels of Light - A Study of the Chakras	Rosalyn L. Bruyere
Your Sixth Sense	Belleruth Naparstek

TAPES AND COMPACT DISCS

Keeper of the Holy Grail, Ascension Harmonics, Light from Assisi, & other music titles; *Richard has dedicated his music to transform-ation and the awakening of inner joy. He also creates beautiful musical soul portraits for individuals, couples and groups..*

Richard Shulman
1-888-699-3682

General Wellness, and a wide range of other Health Journeys guided imagery and affirmation tapes. *Excellent for specific illnesses and emotional concerns. Immerse yourself! – very, very healing.*

Belleruth Naparstek
healthjourneys.com
1-800-800-8661

Dynamic Meditation, Chakra Breathing and other active meditations. *Will clear your energy.* Also many lecture tapes on life. *Thought-provoking!*

Osho
www.osho.org

The Rainbow Breath Meditation. *A great 15 min. grounding pick-me-up and journey through the chakras.*

Ticia Agri
603-778-6247

Workshop tapes on many aspects of healing. *Stimulating & challenging - will stretch you.*

Rosalyn L. Bruyere
rosalynlbruyere.org

LISTENER'S COMMENTS ABOUT *ROOTS & WINGS*

Many listeners have their own story to tell about their experience of the audio:
"Its sound, vibrations and effect are wonderful. I love it!"

"I listened to it on the plane and it brought tears to my eyes as I floated over the Rockies"

"One of the best meditation audios I have heard",

"I got so drawn in to Puja's soothing calming voice that I eventually feel asleep"
                                                                 (*from someone with insomnia*)
"I have listened to *ROOTS & WINGS* practically every day since its release, . . . and I always find something meaningful with each listening. You mention that 'with repeated listening you will build inner strength'. I have certainly found that to be the case."

"My son is 5 and 1/2, and he usually tells me to turn the volume higher so that he can hear the tape too."

"There's such a tone of acceptance and guidance from the heart. It transported me to a very deep place." "It helps me relax my lockjaw condition" . . .

"The flow of the tape is so centered and centering".

"It has brought me great comfort. I listened to it every day after the death of my partner."

"I used it very successfully with my writing group. It helped us get in touch with our own stories"

ABOUT PUJA A. J. THOMSON

Puja Thomson is a counselor, healing facilitator, educator and minister of the Healing Light Center Church, founded by the Reverend Rosalyn Bruyere. For over thirty years she has worked both in the United Kingdom and United States to develop a unique blend of dynamic techniques to transform old patterns and release blocked energy. She skillfully leads individuals and groups to new levels of awareness as she helps them look creatively at the positive side of negative situations and learn to use their energy to welcome change.

For two decades she worked as an educator and training specialist, through institutions in Scotland such as the University of Edinburgh. She was a catalyst for change at local, regional and national levels in the fields of juvenile justice and the interdisciplinary professional training of teachers, social workers and community workers.

Puja has been fed by many roots. From the *Old World* of her youth - its history, lineage and culture, she learned the price of freedom. From the *Ancient Celtic World*, she experienced interdependence with all of nature's great circle of life, and delight in song, poetry, imagination and mystery. In the *Third World* of India and Sri Lanka, she was nourished by the gift of simplicity, - a smile, a flower, life itself. There she was greatly influenced by meditating in the energy field of a Master - Osho. In the *New World* of North America, she learned to hitch her wagon to a star, opening up to new possibilities.

Puja believes that, to meet the challenges of survival, we must carry forward the best of all our roots. To support such a change, she developed a holistic, transformational therapy practice, _ROOTS & WINGS_, that honors the interconnectedness of the body, mind, emotions, and spirit. Her individual sessions, workshops, ceremonies, and healing retreats support individuals in bringing inner and outer healing. Her creative tools include audios, workbooks, and handouts.

Puja Thomson was born and educated in Scotland, and now lives in New York State. She is currently writing a self-help book, *TAKE ROOT, TAKE WING: Using Your Past to Empower Your Future.*

For more information, go to www.rootsnwings.com, e-*mail:* puja@rootsnwings.com *or write:* P.O. Box 1081, New Paltz NY 12561

ACKNOWLEDGEMENTS

This book would not be complete without mention of the many friends who have supported and encouraged me throughout the process of writing this workbook. In particular, I would like to thank three people have been central from start to finish - Janette Black for constant encouragement and a wide range of computer skills, Matthew Fasolino for all manner of practical help and appetizing culinary skills to keep me fortified and my "writing buddy", Miki Frank, for ongoing dialog, editorial suggestions and delightful working dinners.

I am fortunate to have had the backing of members of two monthly groups: the Monday Evening Creative Circle and the Sunday Healing Circle: Kathleen Ellis, Miki Frank, Lyn Mayo, Judy McGrath, Ellen Sribnick; and Angela Balletto, Kathryn Groth, Susan Hanson, Claire Kamp, Cora LeFevre, Kate Lindemann, Kate Loye, June Peoples, Holly Rizzo, Fay Sanders, Lynne Svenningsen, Ma Veet Tamaso, Shirley Pedersen Welden and Susan Wisherd. Thank you, one and all.

My gratitude for timely feedback, clearly and generously given at key moments, goes to Josephine Burns in Scotland, and to Joan Casamo, Kathleen Ellis, Patricia Exman, Janet Hand, Patricia Pfost, Janet Russo and Nina Smiley. Many thanks to Karen and Andy Goldstein for business mentoring and to Donn Smith of Windows Computer Solutions for responding, often at a moment's notice, to all manner of computer glitches.

DEDICATION

I honor my parents, Ena May Ross and John Steven Thomson; my grandparents, Anne Bruce and William Smart Ross, Elizabeth Stevenson and Matthew Thomson as well as their ancestors. I also honor the catalysts for my inner life, especially Dr. Winifred Rushforth, Osho and the Rev. Rosalyn L. Bruyere; and fellow-travelers past and present in Sempervivum, among sannyasins and the children of the Isthmus. All have triggered much change in my life.

As my final entry, **I dedicate** the *ROOTS & WINGS WORKBOOK* to the next generation of Thomsons, Kathleen Vanora Thomson and Fiona Eleanor Thomson, and to the many courageous clients and workshop participants who, by their inner work and actions, contribute to the planetary healing of future generations.

ROOTS & WINGS ORDERING INFORMATION

*To order **ROOTS & WINGS** CDs, tapes and workbooks:*

Visit your local bookstore.
These products are available to bookstores through New Leaf Distributing (Tel:1-800-326-2665;   Fax: 1-800-326-1066;   E-mail: newleaf@newleaf-dist.com)

OR

Send the special order form inserted at the back of the workbook to ROOTS & WINGS, P.O. Box 1081, New Paltz, NY 12561

OR

E-mail puja@rootsnwings.com

BLANK PAGES FOR YOUR CREATIVE USE